Our Favorite Flowers

Ask 20 people their favorite flower.
Show the answers on this bar grap

15										
14										
13										
12										
11										
10										
9										
8										
7										
6										
5										
4										
3										
2										
1										

rose   tulip   daisy

1

Write a verse about kites.

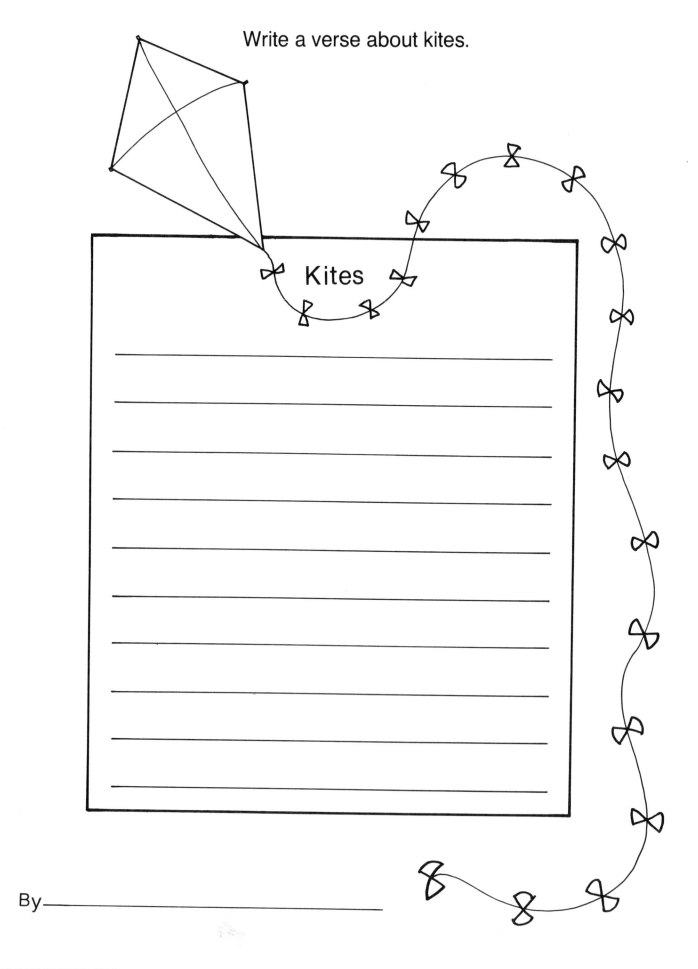

Kites

By_____

March Winds and April Showers

Find the hidden weather words.

```
S U N S H I N E A W I N D B
N C O L W F P N X E P F R Q
O P R E C I P I T A T I O N
W D T E M P E R A T U R E G
F M S T O R M S Y H Z E S R
L I G H T N I N G E I O Q A
A B N U O E L O W R R G T I
K H L R F W G W U H T C H N
E M A R K Z E J D E T L U D
S R A I N T O R N A D O N R
G L G C L D V Y S T U U D O
J A H A C H E M I S T D E P
I K L N I W S W V A X Y R S
B R E E Z E M O I S T U R E
```

_____ breeze
_____ cloudy
_____ dew
_____ fog
_____ gale
_____ hail
_____ heat
_____ high
_____ hurricane

_____ lightning
_____ low
_____ mist
_____ moisture
_____ precipitation
_____ rain
_____ raindrops
_____ showers
_____ sleet

_____ snow
_____ snowflakes
_____ storm
_____ sunshine
_____ temperature
_____ thunder
_____ tornado
_____ weather
_____ wind

Now, put a red x next to each word on the list that describes SPRING weather.

EVAN-MOOR CORP., 1986

SPRING ACTIVITIES

Name It

	flower	something you can buy in a store	something to eat or drink	describing word	boy's name
example L	lily	lock	lemonade	lumpy	Larry
S					
P					
R					
I					
N					
G					

Spring Bouquet

Color:

 yellow   3  blue

 red   2 orange

green

red and white

EVAN-MOOR CORP., 1986

SPRING ACTIVITIES

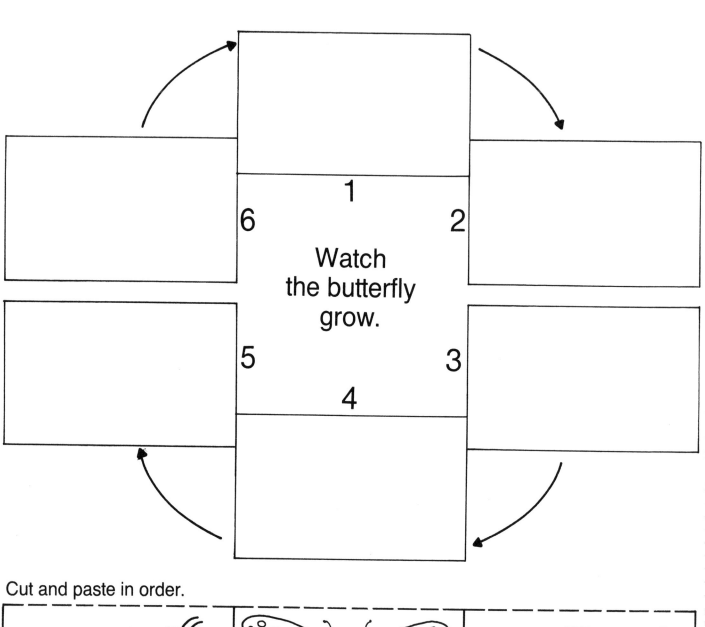

	1	
6	Watch the butterfly grow.	2
5		3
	4	

Cut and paste in order.

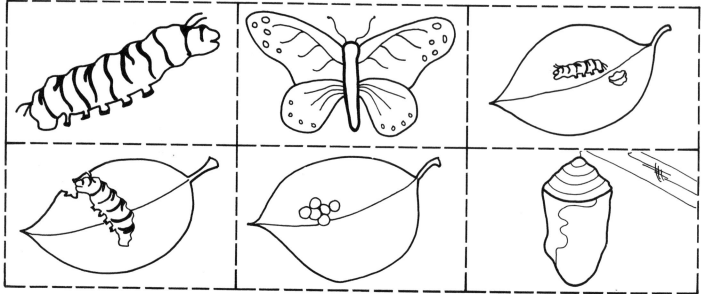

Butterfly Shape Poems

1. Draw.
   Get a piece of paper.
   Use a crayon or pen.
   Draw only the outline of
   the butterfly.

2. Describe the butterfly.
   Get a piece of writing
   paper. Make a list of
   words or phrases about
   the butterfly. Arrange
   them in a way that
   sounds pleasing to you.

small
colorful
curly tongue
can fly
antennae
beautiful
tiny scales
soft
sips nectar

3. Get a sheet of plain
   paper. Put the paper
   over your drawing. Clip
   the papers together with
   a paper clip so they
   won't wiggle. Write your
   description following the
   shape of the picture.

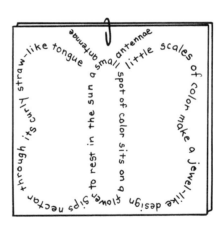

4. Get a sheet of colored
   paper. Paste your poem
   to the paper to make a
   frame.

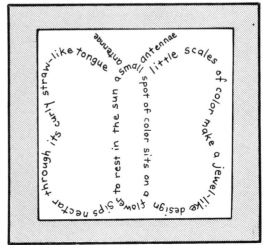

Color. Cut out. Paste to blue paper.

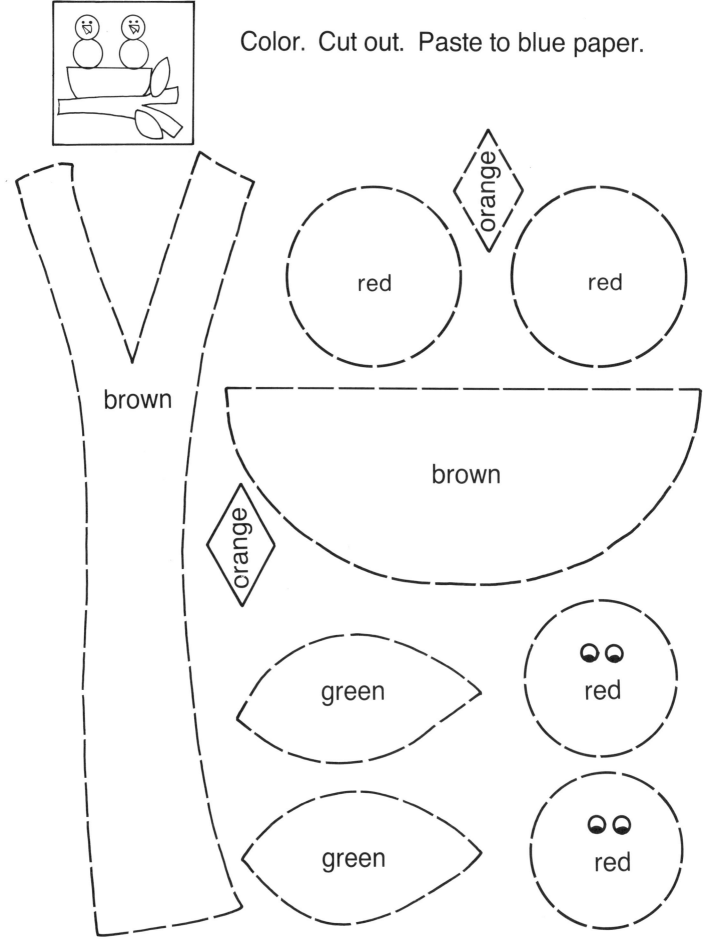

red

orange

red

brown

brown

orange

green

red

green

red

Write a cinquain for spring.

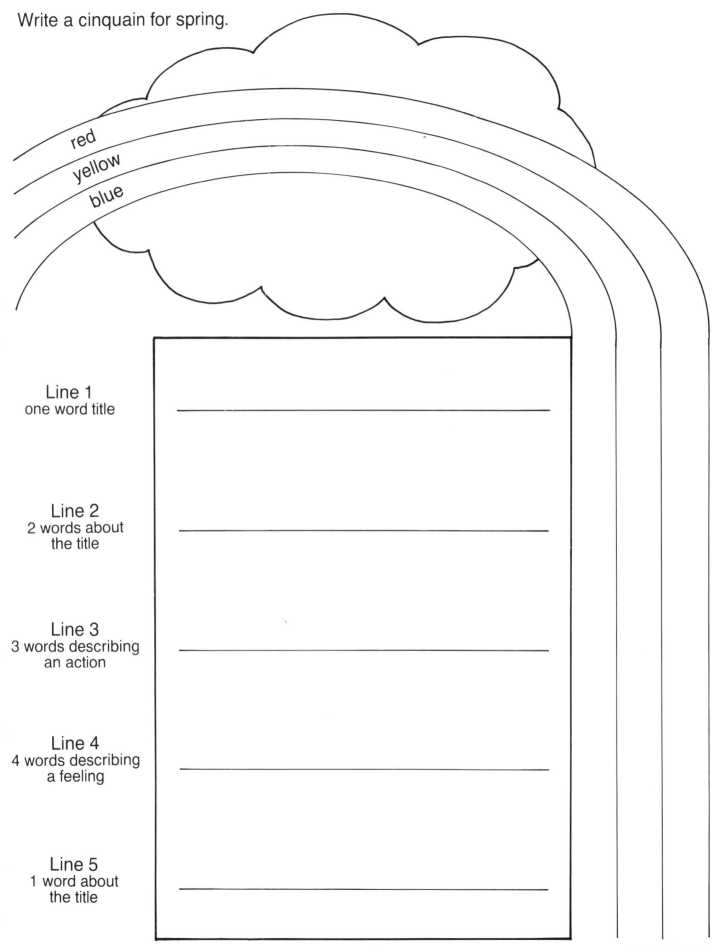

red
yellow
blue

Line 1
one word title

Line 2
2 words about
the title

Line 3
3 words describing
an action

Line 4
4 words describing
a feeling

Line 5
1 word about
the title

Find the 14 animals.

1. Cut.   2. Paste to lined paper.   3. Write.

In _____'s Flower Basket

- Unscramble the flower names. • **You must use all the letters.** • **Check spelling.**
- Write each name on the correct blossom. • **Colour each flower.**

sore   yill   naticaron
liptu   sydai   foddfail
           ypppo

Teacher: Use this form for copying poems, writing letters or creating an original story. Paste a 7½″ X 5″ sheet of lined paper in the center of the border and then reproduce.

How Does Your Garden Grow?

Jack planted a magic bean seed and climbed to the clouds for an exciting adventure. Here is your magic seed. Draw a picture to show what will grow. Then get a sheet of paper and describe your own adventure.

Paste your picture to the top of your story.

Name:

Aunt Mollie's Flower Garden

Aunt Mollie is ready to start planting her spring flower garden, but she spilled all her seed packages. Now they are so mixed up that she can't find which seeds she wants to use. You can help make her job easier by putting them in alphabetical order.

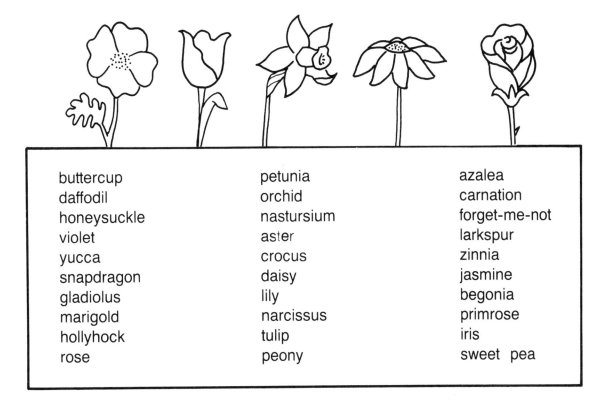

buttercup	petunia	azalea
daffodil	orchid	carnation
honeysuckle	nastursium	forget-me-not
violet	aster	larkspur
yucca	crocus	zinnia
snapdragon	daisy	jasmine
gladiolus	lily	begonia
marigold	narcissus	primrose
hollyhock	tulip	iris
rose	peony	sweet pea

1. _____

2. _____

3. _____

4. _____

5. _____

6. _____

7. _____

8. _____

9. _____

10. _____

11. _____

12. _____

13. _____

14. _____

15. _____

16. _____

17. _____

18. _____

19. _____

20. _____

21. _____

22. _____

23. _____

24. _____

25. _____

26. _____

27. _____

28. _____

29. _____

30. _____

Egg Heads

Make each face different.
Give it a name.
Get a piece of paper.
Write a paragraph about
each new "person."

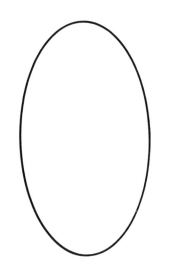

1. _____

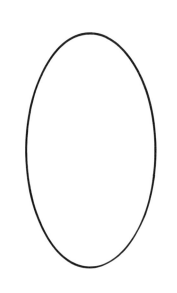

2. _____

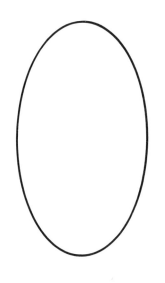

3. _____

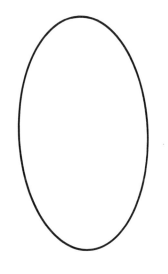

4. _____

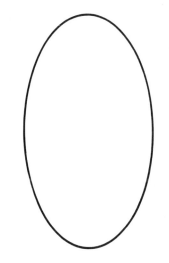

5. _____

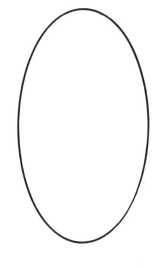

6. _____

Connect the dots. Count by 2's.

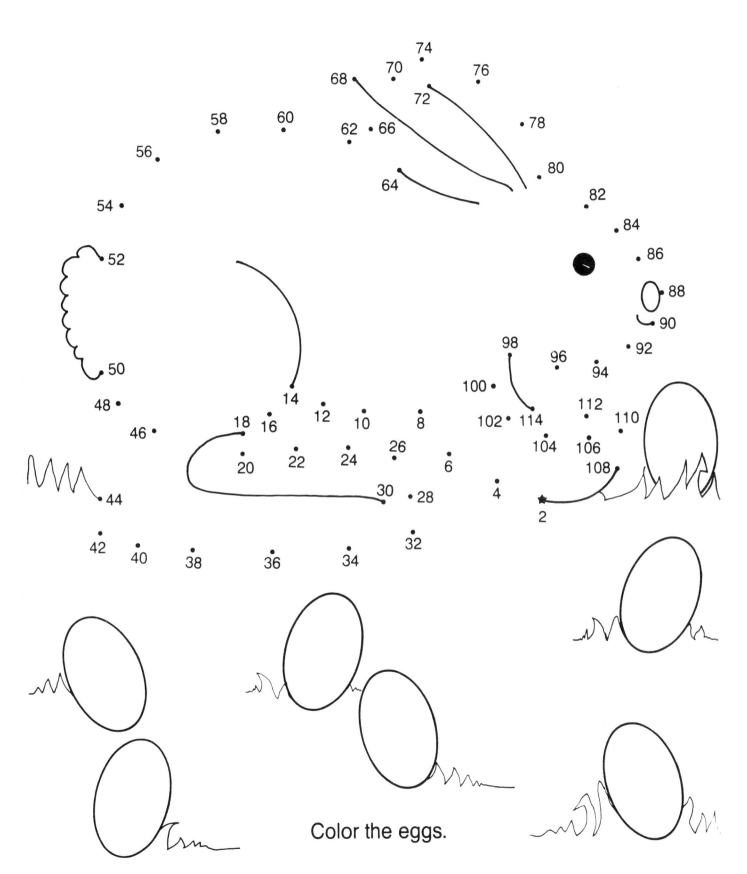

Color the eggs.

Complete the chick in its egg. Color.

Connect the dots to see who is on the nest.
Count by 2's.

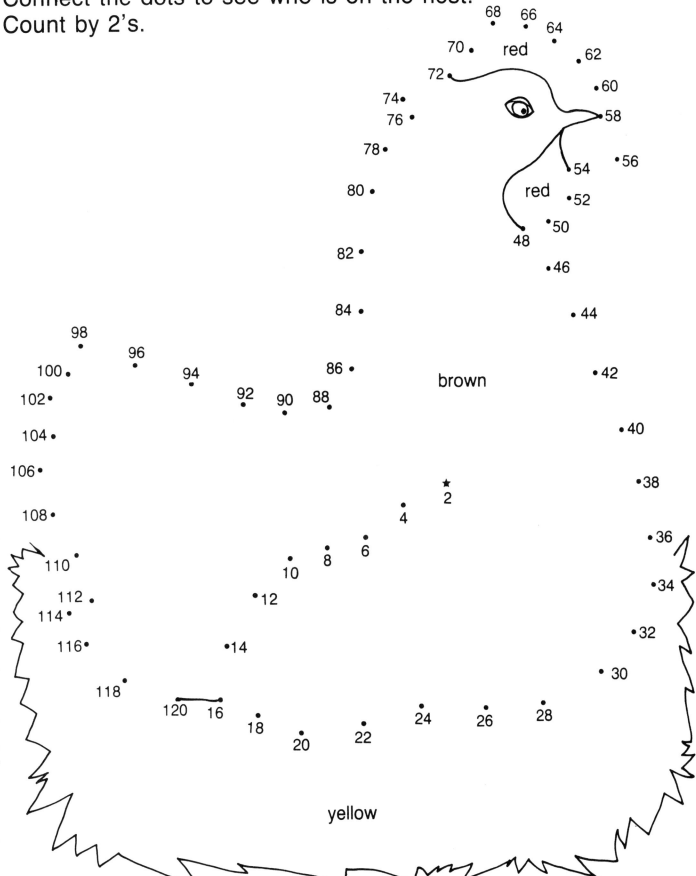

Easter Crossword

Across

2. a spring holiday
4. plant daffodil _____ in the garden
5. send a greeting _____
8. change something from plain to fancy
11. another name for rabbit
12. an Easter hat
14. Easter flowers
15. a green plant covering the ground
16. to look for something

Down

1. to hunt
3. day of the week
4. a container with a handle
6. change the color of something
7. people go to _____ on Sundays
9. another name for bunny
10. a sign for a church
13. hens lay _____

Word Box:

basket	Easter
bonnet	eggs
bulbs	grass
bunny	hunt
card	lilies
church	rabbit
cross	search
decorate	Sunday
dye	

An Easter Surprise

1	moo	baa	clang	buzz / ten	splash	peep / zero	ouch	quack	woof
2	snake	dog	zebra	owl	man	duck	cow	moose	fish
3	Maine	Atlantic	Idaho	Mars / Iowa	Florida	Earth / Texas	Alaska	Pacific	Montana
4	orange	milk	apple	plum / roast	fig / potato	pear / steak	cherry	juice	banana
5	fork	book	pan / log	window	table	bottle	nail / desk	letter	knife
6	feather	toes	fin	mane	gills	hoof	scale	finger	beak
7	tree	buffalo	pig	elk	toad	poodle	duck	whale	carrot
8	rose	worm	dog	monkey	eel	horse	fish	mule	tulip
9	grass	bear	swan	cat	cow	parrot	hen	hippo	cactus
10	bush	bee / weed	deer	mice	moose	canary	frog	ant / corn	vine

Color:

Row 1: sounds-blue
  numbers-red

Row 2: 4 legs-brown
  2 legs-red
  0 legs-blue

Row 3: planets -red
  oceans-brown
  states-blue

Row 4: fruit-blue
  vegetables-yellow
  meat-green
  things to drink-brown

Row 5: wood-yellow
  metal-blue
  glass-green
  paper-brown

Row 6: parts of a:
  horse-green
  fish-yellow
  bird-blue
  person-brown

Rows 7-10: animals-brown
  plants-blue

SPRING ACTIVITIES

1. Color the hare.
2. Cut out all pieces.
3. Put the pieces together with brass fasteners.

A Dancing Hare

An *Eggs...tra* Special Word Search

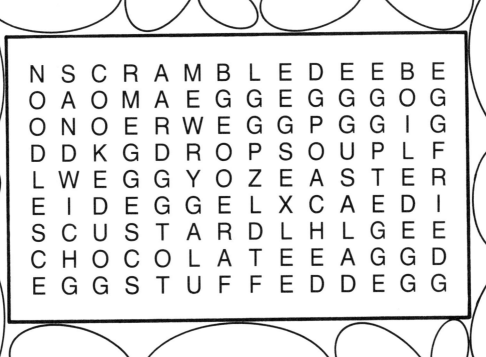

```
N S C R A M B L E D E E B E
O A O M A E G G E G G G O G
O N O E R W E G G P G G I G
D D K G D R O P S O U P L F
L W E G G Y O Z E A S T E R
E I D E G G E L X C A D I
S C U S T A R D L H L G E E
C H O C O L A T E E A G G D
E G G S T U F F E D D E G G
```

Egg _____   _____ eggs

drop soup	raw
salad	scrambled
sandwich	fried
custard	poached
roll	boiled
noodles	stuffed
	Easter
	chocolate
	dyed

NOW...how many times can you find **egg**?

Chicken... Egg... Chicken... Egg

Turn the wheel.
Watch the egg hatch.
See the chicken grow.

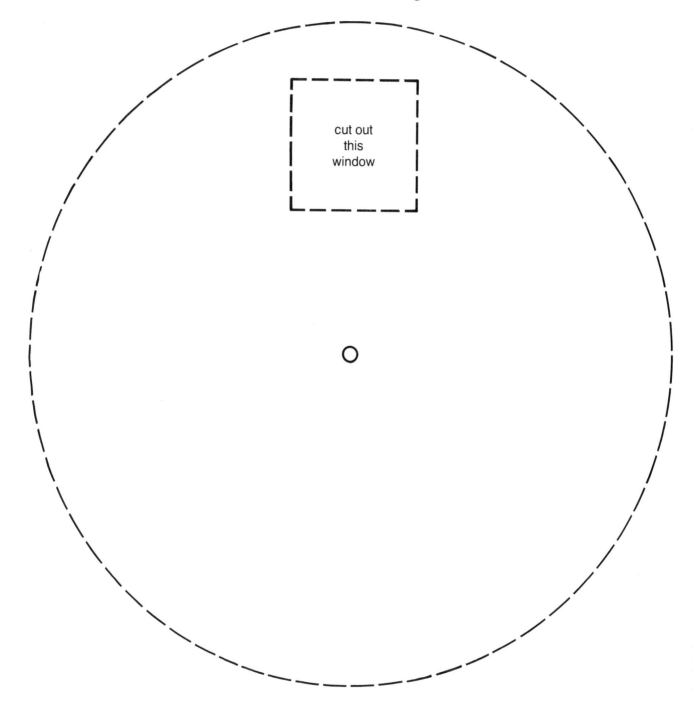

cut out
this
window

1. Cut out both wheels.
2. Color the pictures.
3. Put the two wheels together with a brass paper fastener.

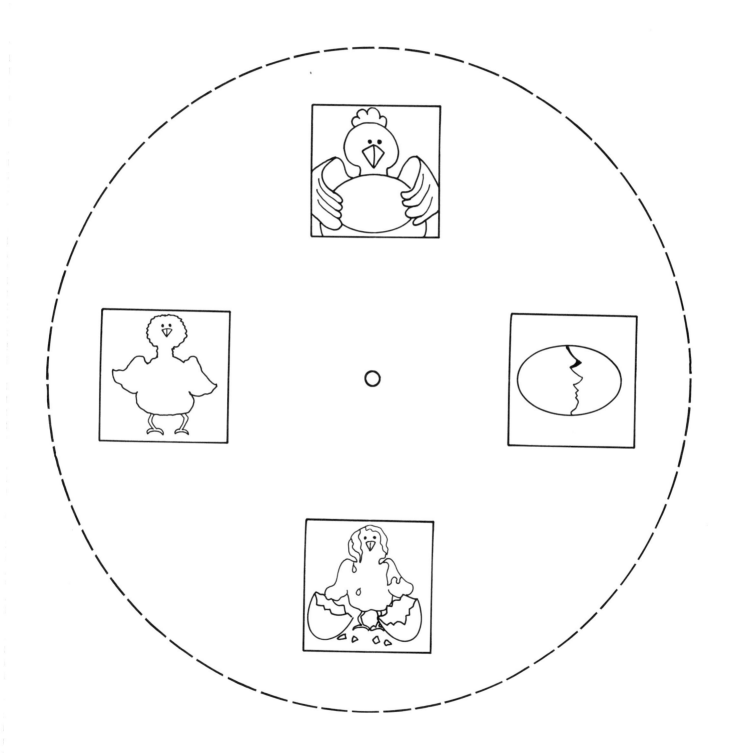

Help Humpty Dumpty put the eggs together.

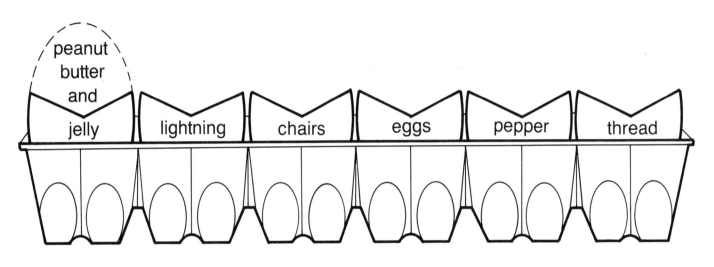

peanut butter and jelly | lightning | chairs | eggs | pepper | thread

toothpaste | mitt | socks | cookies | glove | dogs

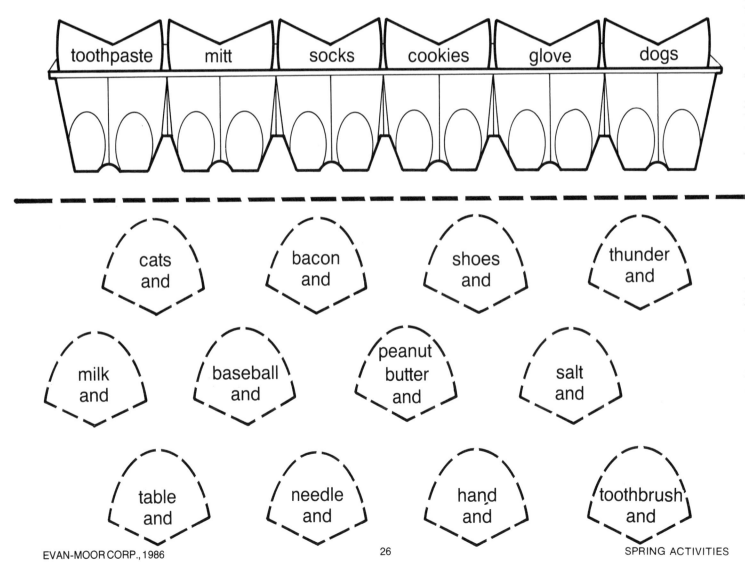

cats and | bacon and | shoes and | thunder and

milk and | baseball and | peanut butter and | salt and

table and | needle and | hand and | toothbrush and

Take a peek under the eggs.

Write an Easter story on your paper.

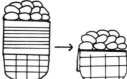

Cut, then paste to the top of a sheet of paper.

Cut, then paste to the bottom of the sheet of paper.

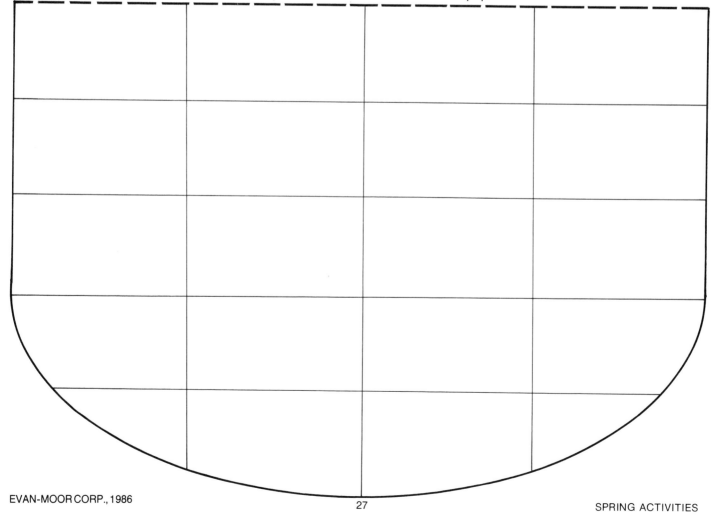

Bunny Tales

1. Choose a title. Copy it on your writing paper.
2. Put your imagination to work.
3. Write a special story.
4. Illustrate your story.

The Forgetful Easter Bunny
Peter Cottontail's First Easter
Arturo and the Mysterious Egg
How the Easter Bunny Gets His Egg
If I Were the Easter Rabbit
Tammy and the Magic Basket
In My Easter Basket
The Substitute Easter Bunny

Pysanky Eggs

Ukrainian Easter eggs are decorated with symbols of good wishes. These beautiful eggs are then given to special friends and family members. Here are some of the symbols used and what they mean:

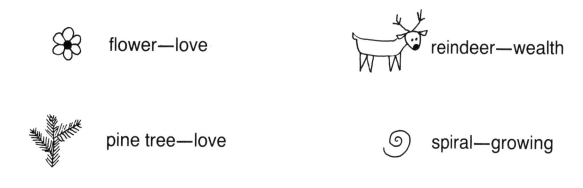

flower—love

reindeer—wealth

pine tree—love

spiral—growing

hen and rooster—wishes coming true

Decorate this egg with an "Easter wish."
Give your egg to a special friend.

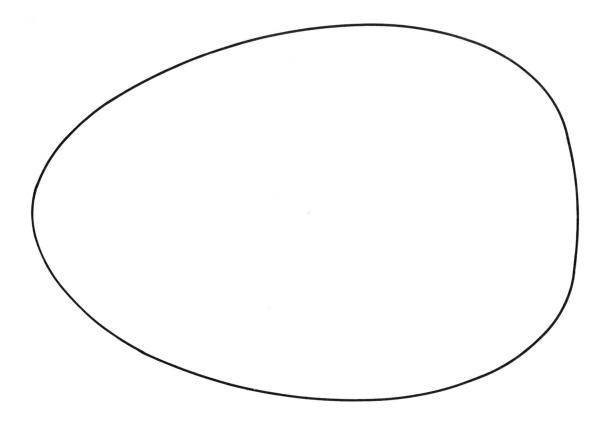

Unscramble the Eggs

Help Mr. Rabbit decorate the Easter eggs.

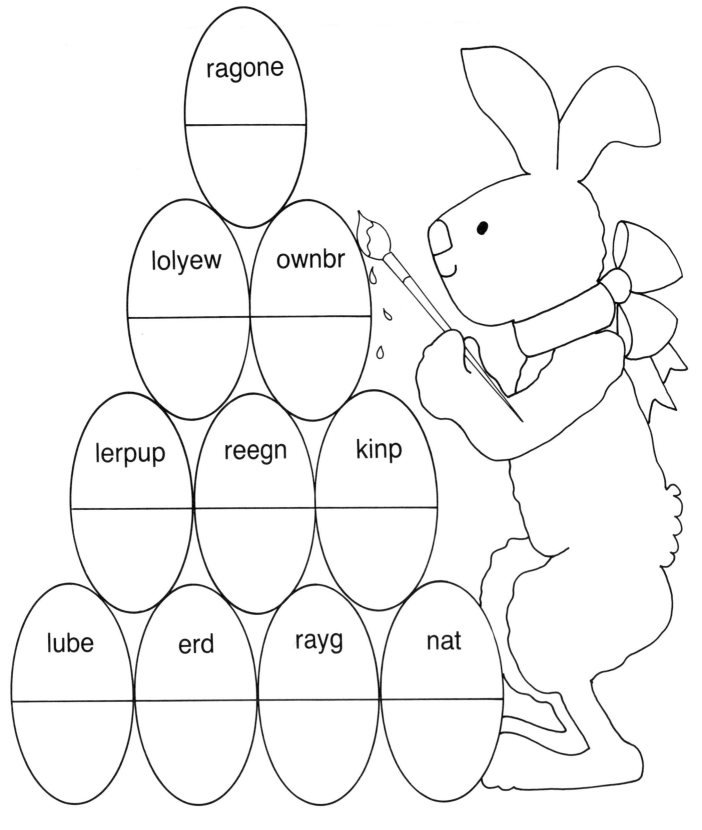

ragone

lolyew   ownbr

lerpup   reegn   kinp

lube   erd   rayg   nat

How to Dye an Easter Egg

Color the picture.

1.

2.

3.

4.

- -

Cut. Paste in order.

Put eggs in the cups. Turn the eggs with a spoon.

Get cups and spoons. Set them on the table.

Lift the eggs out and let them dry.

Put dye in each cup. Add water and vinegar. Stir.

Easter Egg Puzzles

Put the puzzle pieces together to find the hidden animals.

1. Cut   2. Paste to a sheet of paper.   3. Color

A Rabbit Fantasy—Read and Draw

Horace Hare

Not all rabbits are soft and cuddly. Horace Hare has a terrible disposition. He can't get along with any of the other animals and is always up to mischief.

Get a sheet of paper and draw this evil-tempered hare. Let your picture show what kind of mischief Horace gets into.

Jake Jackrabbit

Jake has had a miserable day. First he was chased by a hungry fox, then he fell into a muddy puddle while trying to escape.

Get a sheet of paper and draw Jake *after* his mishap. You may want to include the hungry fox in your picture.

Big Bad Bart Bunny

Bart's parents were very surprised when their cute little bundle of fur continued to grow and grow and grow until he reached 6 feet 4 inches and 250 pounds. Today he supports his huge appetite by wrestling professionally.

Get a sheet of paper and draw Big Bad Bart in his championship bout.

Lillie Lop-Ears

Lillie was always an exceptionally lovely rabbit. Her silky ears fell down in the charming way of all lop-ears, her little pink nose wiggled delightfully, while her dark eyes sparkled like twinkling stars. Lillie has become the star of T.V. and the movies. This week her picture was on the cover of *Today in T.V.* magazine.

Get a sheet of paper and draw the lovely Lillie on the magazine cover.

Easter Egg Hunt

Color the hidden eggs.

How many eggs? _____

Little Brown Bunny Bag

Follow these directions to make a bunny bag for yourself or for a little friend.

1. Take a brown lunch bag.

2. Cut out ears.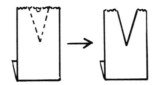

3. Draw and color:
   - pink ears
   - black eyes
   - black nose
   - a little mouth

4. Add: black paper whiskers
   a cotton tail

5. Staple the ears together. Open the bag.

    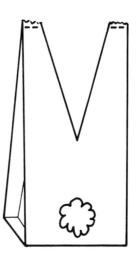

Mushroom Mysteries

Paste the riddle to the top of the mushroom it answers.

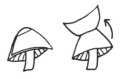

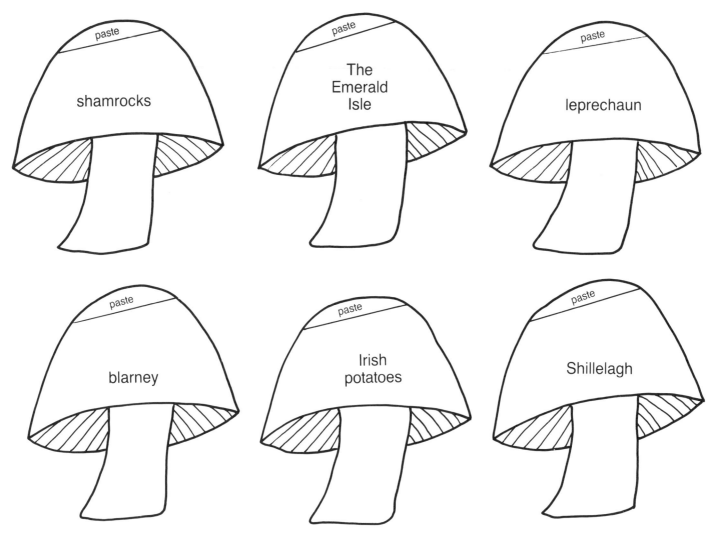

shamrocks

The Emerald Isle

leprechaun

blarney

Irish potatoes

Shillelagh

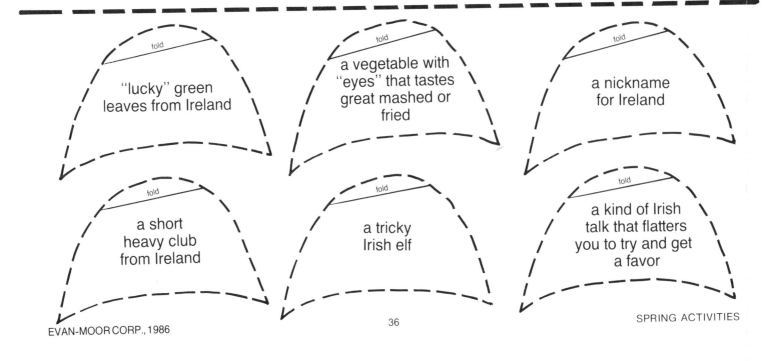

"lucky" green leaves from Ireland

a vegetable with "eyes" that tastes great mashed or fried

a nickname for Ireland

a short heavy club from Ireland

a tricky Irish elf

a kind of Irish talk that flatters you to try and get a favor

EVAN-MOOR CORP., 1986

SPRING ACTIVITIES

1. Draw the picture.
2. Cut out the pictures.

3. Paste each picture to lined paper.
4. Write.

a brave rabbit	a forgetful Leprechaun
a magic egg	a lazy chick
the end of the rainbow	a strange garden

My Lucky Shamrock
What can it be?

Write a wish on each section...

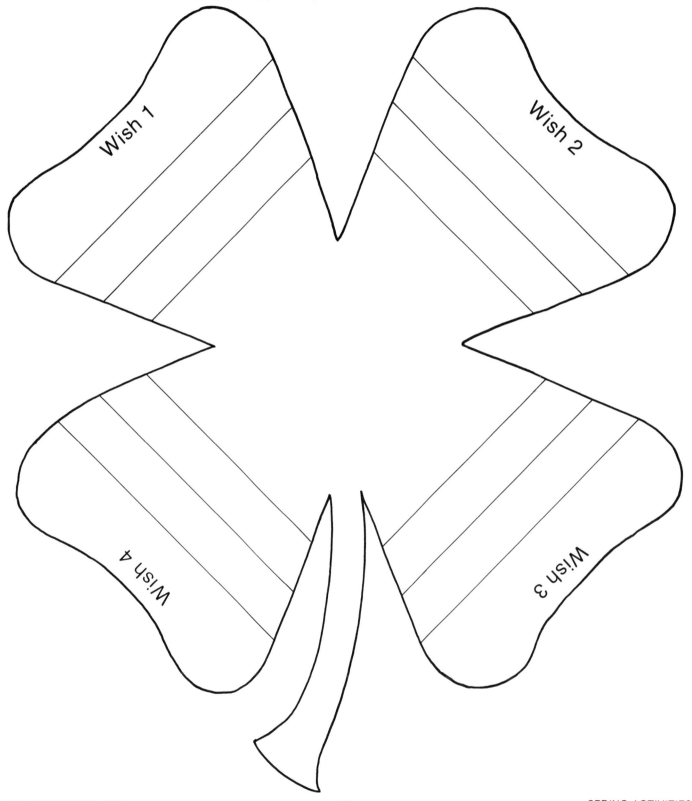

Complete the leprechaun   Color.

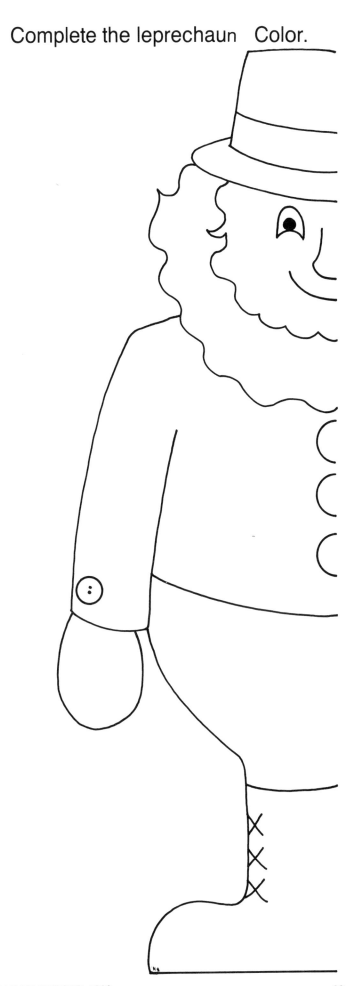

Help the Leprechaun find the hidden words.

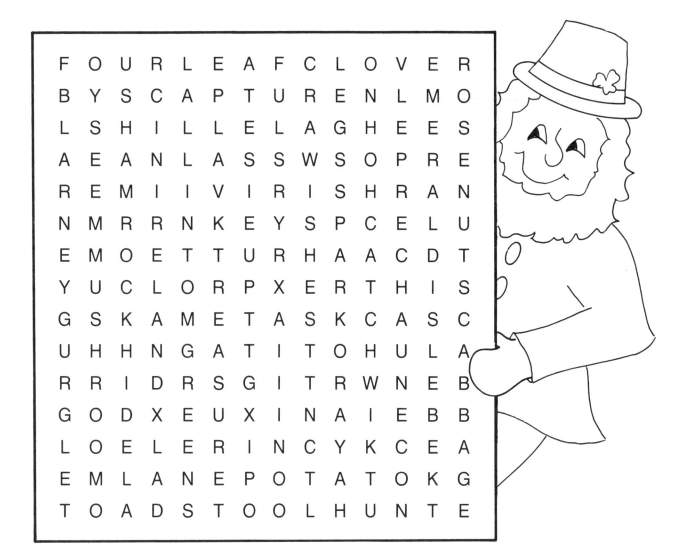

```
F O U R L E A F C L O V E R
B Y S C A P T U R E N L M O
L S H I L L E L A G H E E S
A E A N L A S S W S O P R E
R E M I I V I R I S H R A N
N M R R N K E Y S P C E L U
E M O E T T U R H A A C D T
Y U C L O R P X E R T H I S
G S K A M E T A S K C A S C
U H H N G A T I T O H U L A
R R I D R S G I T R W N E B
G O D X E U X I N A I E B B
L O E L E R I N C Y K C E A
E M L A N E P O T A T O K G
T O A D S T O O L H U N T E
```

blarney	hide	potato
cabbage	hunt	Saint Patrick
capture	Ireland	shamrock
catch	Irish	shillelagh
Emerald Isle	lad	silver
Erin	lass	tiny
four-leaf clover	Leprechaun	toadstool
gold	magic	treasure
green	mushroom	wee
		wishes

Can you find any other words? _____ If yes, how many? _____

Story Starters

1. Choose a story starter.
2. Paste it to the top of a sheet of paper.
3. Write!
4. Draw a picture to go with your story.

All his life Timothy had heard that leprechauns hide their fortunes. He was determined to locate some of that treasure. All he had to do was capture one of the tiny green fellows.

I never realized how exciting my family's vacation in Ireland was going to be, until . . .

One spring evening, Tonya spied a wee leprechaun racing across her backyard. She . . .

Riddle Time

Use the Morse code to solve these riddles.

A ·—	E ·	I ··	M ——	Q ——·—	U ··—	Y —·——
B —···	F ··—·	J ·———	N —·	R ·—·	V ···—	Z ——··
C —·—·	G ——·	K —·—	O ———	S ···	W ·——	
D —··	H ····	L ·—··	P ·——·	T —	X —··—	

1. How does a leprechaun make gold soup?

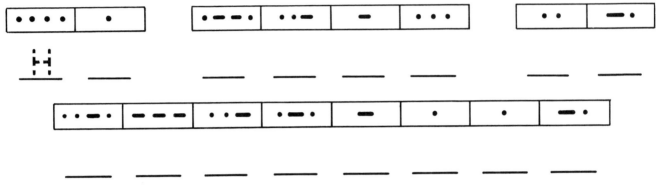

2. Why did the elephant paint himself green?

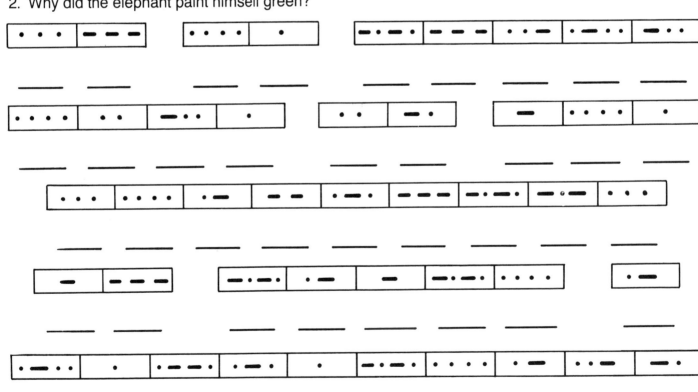

Note: Student will need an 8½″ X 15″ sheet of colored construction paper.

May Basket

1. Fold your colored paper in half.
2. Place your pattern on the fold and cut - - - lines.
3. Push side folds inside basket and paste the sides shut.
4. Make a design on your basket.

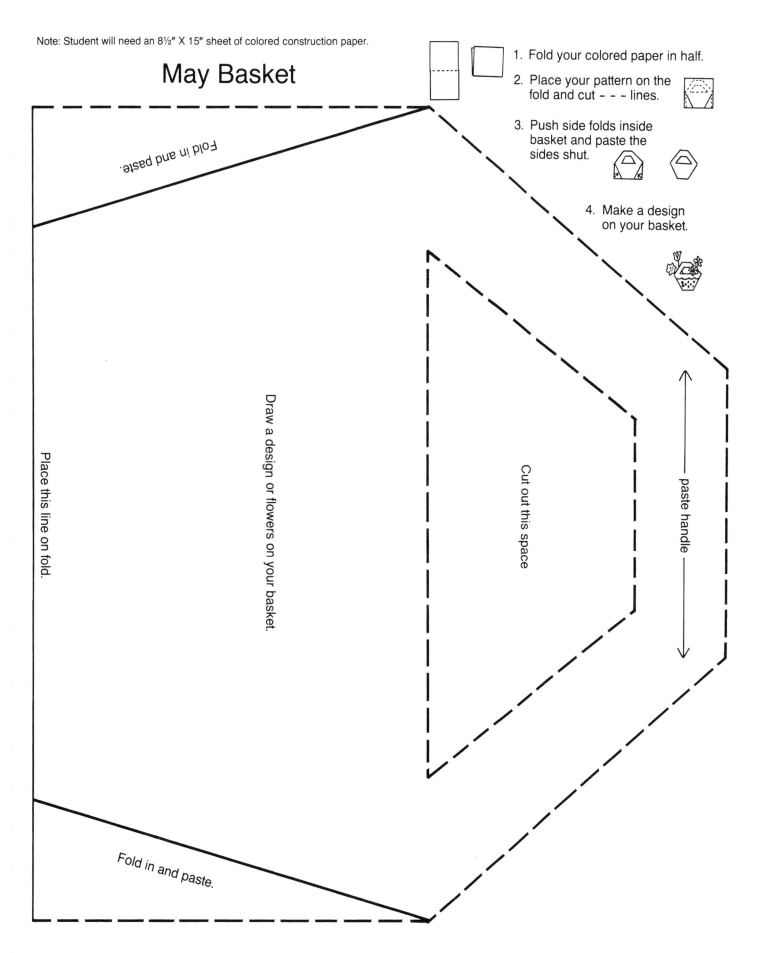

Fold in and paste.

Fold in and paste.

Place this line on fold.

Draw a design or flowers on your basket.

Cut out this space

paste handle

Fill your basket with flowers.
Hang the basket on a friend's front door for a May Day Surprise.

SPRING ACTIVITIES

Dance Around the Maypole

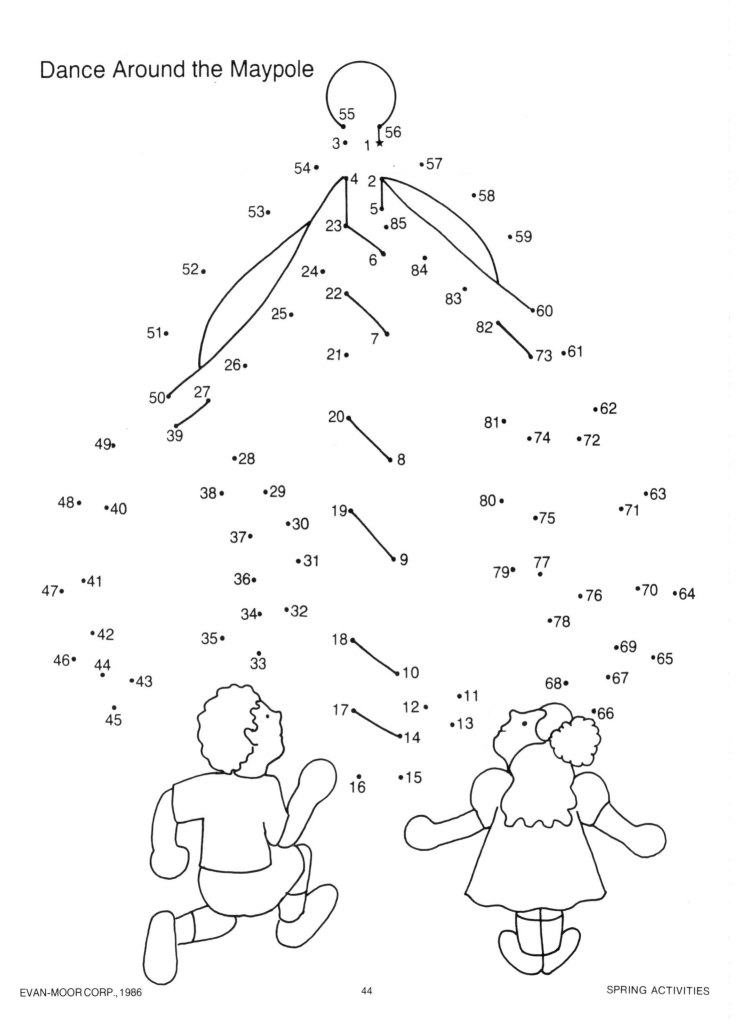

Cut and paste the puzzle.

_____'s Mother

Draw a picture of your mother inside this frame.

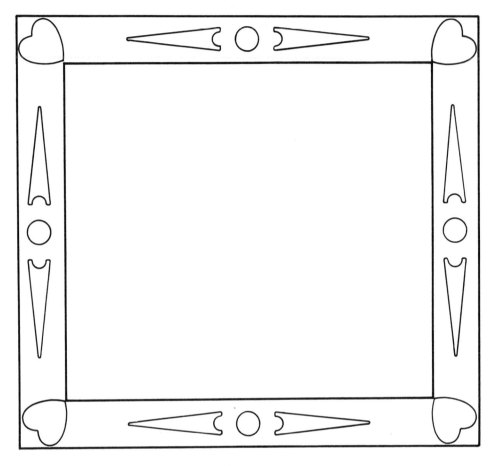

Now, write a description of why she is special.

_____

_____

_____

_____

_____

_____

A Bear-y Special Mother's Day Card

1. Take a 6 inch by 9 inch piece of paper.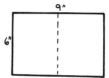

2. Fold the paper in half.

3. Draw a little bear on the outside.

4. Write this message on the card:

    Outside: This little bear
              is here to say...

    Inside: I love you Mother
              EVERY DAY!

5. Sign your name and carry the card home to your own special mother.

A Report About _____
your mother's name

Interview your mother to find the information you don't know.

Part 1: A Description
> Write a paragraph telling what your mother looks like. Make it clear and complete.

Part 2: Her Childhood
> Write one or two paragraphs about when your mother was a girl. Include when and where she was born, what it was like where she lived growing up, her likes and dislikes and any other interesting information about that time in her life.

Part 3: As An Adult
> Write one or more paragraphs about your mother now. Include her job, her special interests and talents and what she likes and dislikes now.

Part 4: Write a paragraph explaining why your mother is special.

Copy your report neatly. You may want to include a picture of your mother as a child and as an adult.